Bewildered Minds

Commoner's Tale

Girish Pillai

BookLeaf Publishing

India | USA | UK

Made with ❤ on the BookLeaf Publishing Platform
www.bookleafpub.in
www.bookleafpub.com

Dedication

To my parents, whose love laid the foundation for everything I am.

And to my wife "my wonder woman "

When the world crumbled around me, when the weight of life felt too heavy to bear, you stood by my side, unwavering and fearless. Your love, strength, and belief in me became the light that led me through the darkest of days.

This book exists because you never let me give up.

This is as much yours as it is mine.

Preface

This book holds fragments of truth - not just from my own life, but from the silent struggles and quiet victories that echo in the life of every common soul. Each poem within these pages carries a part of my story, stitched together with the thread of experiences we all share in one way or another.

As an amateur writer, I found myself not only trying to give voice to my thoughts but also learning to navigate the raw, unpredictable journey of life itself. This book faced its own share of delays, often put on hold by the weight of my real-life struggles. There were moments when giving up felt easier than moving forward.

But in those moments, when the world seemed to collapse around me, there was one constant - my wonder woman, my wife. She stood beside me when the ground beneath us shook, taking the fall with me, without ever asking for anything in return. Her unwavering support, her quiet strength, and her endless belief in me gave me the courage to finish what I started.

This book, in many ways, is as much a tribute to her love and resilience as it is a reflection of my journey. I hope that as you turn these pages, you find a piece of your own story within them and remember that even in our deepest struggles, we are never truly alone.

Acknowledgements

First and foremost, I would like to express my heartfelt gratitude to my family and friends. Your constant encouragement, love, and support have been the pillars that held me up throughout this journey. Every word written, every page completed, was made possible because of your unwavering belief in me.

Most importantly, I owe a special thanks to my wife - my anchor and my guiding light. You have been so much more than just a support; you became my mentor, my inspiration, and the voice that reminded me to trust my own journey. Your faith in me never wavered, even when mine did, and for that, I am eternally grateful.

I would also like to extend my sincere thanks to BookLeaf Publishing for offering me this exciting challenge and creating a platform that inspires writers to think beyond their limits. Your belief in nurturing creativity has helped me take a dream and turn it into reality.

This book is not just a collection of words - it is a reflection of the many souls who walked beside me, guided me, and lifted me when I needed it most. Thank you, from the bottom of my heart.

What's the concern?

A family of four, but one to strive,
Eight hands in all, just two alive.
She bore the weight, while he stood still,
What is the worry? What breaks the will?
Is it wrong for her to wear the crown,
While he just watches the sun go down?

What began as need, then turned to ease,
Now draped in silk, a life to please.
What is the worry? What feeds the flame?
Is it hunger for more or just the name?
Does greed grow swift, or do we swell,
With wants too deep, too hard to quell?

To age was never in the plan,
To live for self-denied, we ran.
With eyes on others, hearts on hold,
What is the worry? What truth is told?
Are there no doors, or none we try,

Do we stay grounded, forgetting to fly?

Why did I grow, with weight so wide?
Innocence lost, like ebbing tide.
Yet still they say, "Not grown enough,"
What is the worry? Why's it so tough?
Did I grow wrong or not at all?
Was I too quick to heed the call?

In between the crowd I was standing alone,
Looking beyond the sea of hurdles,
Every individual trying to live their own dream,
Fighting their own battles, travelling in the boat of hope,
What's the concern?
We are trying to live our dream? Or we are still standing
alone?

Do the whispers in the dark redefine our stride?
Carrying burdens while wearing a mask of pride,
Each smile a façade, each laugh a disguise,
What's the concern?
Are we living for others, or seeking our own skies?

In shadows of doubt, we craft our own fate,
Measured by success while we question our state,
Searching for meaning in the echoes of choice,
Is there freedom in silence, in finding our voice?

Brought Happiness

I tumbled upon my old diary,
Between the torn pages, a well-preserved note,
A note by my father,
A wave of memories swash upon my heart,
My inner child jumped with joy,
Oh yes!!! That was enough to bring back my happiness,

Happiness which I was searching for long time,
Happiness that I had been trying to find in my car,
In my luxury watch, my luxury house, in my utterly
useless things,
A simple piece of paper brought back my happiness,
My vigorously piled up money couldn't buy, was
brought by a simple note.

The note wasn't long and meticulously emotional,
It was simple and read "I will always love you my kid"
Yes, a simple note any father would write to his kid,
My hands were holding it so tight,

Fingers talking to each other, let's unite to bring him this happiness,

My eyes filled with a sea of emotions,
Eyelids struggling to remain open,
Thinking of my old man and how much he loves me,
For a second, I had traveled back to my childhood,
Saw my old man with the same old shirt he has been wearing since I was born,

His same old torn shoes but he was happy,
He was happy to buy me those expensive toys,
He was happy to lift me up,
The same old man!!!
Sorry, the same old father who brought me happiness.

And in that moment, I understood the truth,
That wealth and toys are just fleeting shadows,
While love, a simple note, is the brightest light,
A treasure that glows in the darkest of nights.
Tomorrow's worries fade like the dust in the air,
As I cling to those words, feeling his love everywhere.
So I'll carry this note, a bond across time,
A reminder that happiness is truly sublime.

Bond made by arrangements

Bond born from compromises,
Bond tied by unspoken promises,
Bond that weather countless storms,
Still, they endure! Bonds made by arrangement,

Leading to a life unknown,
Leading to a life uncertain,
Leading to a life of struggles,
Still, it continues! Bond made by arrangement,

Fights over silly issues,
Fights over self-centered attitude,
Fights over other people's life,
Still, they remain! Bond made by arrangement,

She wore the financial tag,
He wore the house tag,
Judgmental society started giving verdicts,
Still, they cherish! Bond made by arrangement,

They searched for serene but chaos haunted them,
They searched for abundance but impoverished haunted them,
They searched for refinement but defilement haunted them,
Still, they remain! Bond made by arrangement,

Through trials and triumphs, they thread,
Through tears and laughter, unsaid,
Through dreams postponed and hopes restored,
Still, they thrive! Bond made by arrangement,

For love might grow where duty reigns,
For partnership blossoms amidst the pains,
For stories unfold, unique and profound,
Still, they remain! Bond made by arrangement.

Make ends meet

Life is harsh on me,
Hurdles have been my soulmate,
Struggles have been my constant partner,
Thus, the question Why me?
Why me not able to make ends meet?

Problems grow with me,
Money struggles to nurture,
Expenses make their own way,
Thus, the question why me?
Why me not able to make ends meet?

Responsibility was born with me,
Lone warrior was based on me,
Fighting was not an option it was survival,
Thus, the question why me?
Why me not able to make ends meet?

Worshipping continued but prayer never answered,
Calling continued but no one answered,

Why I became a self-portrayed Abhimanyu,
Thus, the question why me?
Why me not able to make ends meet?

Heaven and hell both are here,
Karma is what I believe,
Challenges carve stories upon my soul,
Lessons are etched where anguish stole,
Why me, I often cry to the skies,

But strength is born as my truth defies.
Path unlit, yet I find my way,
Through shadows that turn night to day.
Why me, I ask when the weight won't cease,
Yet I rise seeking moments of peace.

Abhimanyu's scars may mirror mine,
Yet in wounds, resilience will shine.
Why me, I wonder through life's demand,
Yet I stride holding dreams in my hand.

The wheel of karma spins and turns,
From every spark a fire burns.
Why me becomes why not,
I dare, For hope still whispers in the air.

In the echoes of doubt, my heart takes flight,

A flicker of courage ignites the night.
With every stumble, my spirit does mend,
In the tapestry woven, I claim my end.

Though storms may rage in a tempestuous sea,
I clutch the horizon, my spirit set free.
The journey unfolds with each step I tread,
Through challenges faced, my fears I shred.

Why me, I ponder, yet here I still stand,
With a warrior's heart and dreams at command.
Life's canvas is painted with colors so bright,
In the dance of resilience, I find my light.

Twisted couple

Caught a glimpse of her,
She was short and I was tall for her,
She was fire and I had patience for her,
Story of twisted couple begins here,

Lazy me meet lazy her,
Story begins with close-up on her,
Curly hair, attitude and dancing with grace,
That what defines her not her face,

She is straight so does her attitude,
She likes real people not fake,
She is strong like nothing can shake,
On the flip side give her a break,

Let's talk about him, he who is easy,
Flirty but not too cheesy,
He was dark with beard,
That's what she liked not his hair,

She was curvy and he was slim,
A contrast that made their story brim,
Opposites collided, sparks blew bright,
They danced through days, argued through night.

He loved her fire, she loved his calm,
Together they found a soothing balm,
Twists and turns marked their tale,
Yet through it all, their love prevailed.

Though lazy, they shared a dream,
Building a life, as a seamless team,
Her grace, his charm a blend divine,
Two souls, tangled but intertwined.

Quiet War

After a longtime, I let my guard down,
Not for the fear I might fall,
For merely that battle lingered long,
Souls adorned in borrowed valor,
They laughed as I bled from a lowered cover.

Bleeding was not my defeat,
Wounds may fade like a passing storm,
Like seasons, souls may drift and bolt,
I stood alone, and alone I may yet stand,
That's not my defeat, I'll rise and bloom as planned

I chose a kindred soul to fight along,
Knowing the warrior would never fail me,
Ran into the battle where blame like arrows flew,
Trust, love, care and empathy everything was on line,
The only soul I trusted trailed behind.

In battle's storm, my calm was torn,
My shield of patience, worn and shorn,

An arrow sharp, of blame and grief,
Struck deep and stole my soul's relief.

Then came a warrior, fierce and true,
Whose grace in fight I always knew,
She stood beside me, brave and fast
Through triumph bright and trial vast,
In loss and win, she gave her the best.

She spoke no words, yet hearts aligned,
Her strength became a guide for mine,
Through shadowed paths and morning light,
She was my flame, my fiercest knight.

When silence screamed and hope ran dry,
She taught me how to rise and try,
No crown she wore, no fane she sought,
Yet battles bowed to all she brought.

Now peace has dawned where war once lay,
But still, I feel her strength each day,
A warrior not just forged in strife,
She was the soul that saved my life.

Being Called Human

Born a human, so they said,
Yet now I walk a path misled.
Flesh and bone like beast and bird,
Yet another word in my mind.

A mind that reached for something more,
For kinship, meaning, myths of yore,
Still I roamed, untamed, alone,
A thinking beast, yet not full-grown.

Greed and rage took root in me,
Taught and twisted endlessly.
I walked as if above the rest,
Head held high, a swollen chest.

Yet blind to all that lies beneath,
The humble ground, the silent grief,
Still I cling to that old name,
"Human," wrapped in fragile flame.

Me, myself my constant song,
Echoed loud, though deeply wrong.
Draped in ego, bare within,
A hollow pride, a painted skin.

We built our walls and named it grace,
A fractured, cold, and crowded place.
Worse than beasts, yet still we claim
The noble echo of that name.

"Human" spoken with no shame.

We feast as one, yet stand apart,
With borrowed hands and hardened heart.
We preach of equals, just and fair
Yet none will truly, freely share.

What are we, behind the name?
A branded ghost, a fleeting flame.
"Human" hollow, worn with pride,
A mask we wear, with truth denied.

Even gods have watched this play,
While we carved faiths to lose our way.
Built our walls of creed and lore,
Yet hungered still for nature's core.

We'll feast on earth, consume its breath,
And name it "growth," though sown with death.
We raise the banner, stake our claim
Progress wrapped in smoke and flame.

Good old chaps

They said "I'm with you", a sweetened lie,
Wrapped in sugar, masked from the eye,
As a child, I held it nearby,
A dream of closeness, warm and clear,
A hope for hands that'd always stays,
To walk beside me, come what may.

Loud voices, yet hollow advice,
Hearts once golden, now cold as ice,
"I'm fine", I say, though not quite true,
Still chasing bonds, I never knew,
Among millions, I remain,
Yearning for friends but grasping pain.

Old friends gather, soft and slow,
With tales the years still gently know,
Laughter tangled in blush and grin,
Moments lost, yet held within.
No friends quite like the ones before
Time worn bonds we still adore.

A circle close, not vast in size,
Yet held the world behind their eyes.
Through storm and sun, they did not stray,
They stood beside me, come what may.
In rise and fall, they bore my name,
Unchanged, unwavering, still the same.

A bond may fade, but memories cling,
In every laugh, in every sting,
In fractured days, their light would shine,
Though paths may twist and time divide,
With every parting, something grows,
A garden where forgotten shows,

"For friendship, Is a tender place where love still grows".

Lone Warrior

In the mirror, my form, my truth resonates.
I carve my journey, stone by stone,
With confidence bold, I walk alone.
With eager soul and open mind,
A seeker's path is what you'll find.

"I can, I will" that's my decree,
Not what the world may claim of me.
Let whispers fly, let judgments fall,
They touch me not, I stand tall.
Through trials faced and lessons learned,
My inner fire ever burned.

I'm here to leave a blazing trace,
To run my path, to win my race.
No fear can shake, no doubt can bend,
I rise, I grow, I don't pretend.
Unstoppable, I forge ahead,
By dreams I'm led, not by dread.

A phoenix I am, through flames I ascend,
Burn me down, I rise again.
Hate if you must, it won't define,
Your shade can't dim this light of mine.
I choose my joy, I hold it tight,
And in that joy, I find my light.

Step forth with fire, embrace the way,
Let change arise, don't drift, don't stay.
Break every chain, let courage swell—
You are the hero—believe, rebel.

Let storms arrive, let chaos scream,
They cannot steal this living dream.
For every scar, a tale I bear,
Of battles braved, of how I care.
I wear my truth like warrior's skin,
With every fall, I rise again.

My voice is thunder, calm and clear,
Not shaped by doubt, nor ruled by fear.
Each breath I take, a vow I make—
To never dim, to never fake.
The world may twist, the tides may turn,
But I remain—alive, and burn.

The climb is steep, the night is long,

But in my chest, a battle song.
A rhythm born from strength and pain,
A melody that won't be chained.
And though alone this road may be,
It's lit by flames that rise from me.

Compulsion of becoming

Born with limbs so small, so slight,
Yet asked to walk with all my might.
A tender mind, so fresh, so new,
Still burdened with a thinker's view,
And taught to speak before I knew.

The world pressed down with silent haste,
To grow up fast, no time to waste.
To answer questions deep and wide,
Before my words could even glide.
I smiled, I laughed, I tried to play,
But forceful hands pulled joy away.

I found my steps, I found my voice,
But learning now was not a choice.
No time to pause, reflect, or see
The wonder of becoming me.
Each win was met with just one plea:
"Now do more, be more, endlessly."

Oh, let me breathe, and learn, and be,
To wander through my path carefree.
What's meant for me will find its place,
I need not win some endless race.
Let me dance within the now,
Not chase a fate I can't allow.

Now learned, adorned with scholar's grace,
Yet bound to join the endless race.
No pause allowed, no space to breathe,
Just climb and climb with dreams beneath.
"Earn more," they said, "be more, achieve!"
No room to stop, no time to grieve.

The weight of work, a golden chain,
Status prized above the strain.
No talk of joy, no time for light,
Just titles chased through sleepless night.
A silent trade of soul for pride,
With happiness cast to the side.

I thought at last the game was done,
The race was run, the prize was won.
Their dreams fulfilled, their silence earned,
At last, I'd live the life I yearned.
But fate had plans not mine to claim,
A new bond formed, yet not the same.

Just as I reached for dreams my own,
Another path by force was shown.
Love, perhaps but shaped by law,
A vow, a tie, a binding flaw.
And marriage came, not as a song,
But as another right from wrong.

The vows were made, the partner near,
I hoped for calm, for skies to clear.
A fresh new page, a softer light,
Perhaps, at last, the world felt right.
But dreams gave way to silent ache,
The joy I sought began to break.

The questions came in whispered tones,
New chains were forged with different stones.
No peace to breathe, no space to mend,
Just pressure dressed as love again.
"When will you bear?" the voices pressed,
A womb, it seemed, was life's new test.

The circle turned, began anew,
With just one cry, the old winds blew.
The same old questions found fresh ground,
This time in the child I'd crowned.
I longed for peace, a softer shore

But found the weight I knew before.

I held my breath, my voice grew thin,
Still dancing to another's hymn.
Their hopes, their rules my silent song,
The pressure stayed, relentless, strong.
Compelled to mold, to play the part,
With little space to guard my heart.

When will it end, this ceaseless strain?
When will I break this heavy chain?
When will I rise to chase my skies,
And find the dreams that I disguise?
When will I breathe, just for my soul,
And live the life that makes me whole?

Loafing

They call it lazy - this stillness, this peace,
A Day spent at home, a soul's sweet release.
No rush, no race, just quiet and slow,
Let them judge - what do they know?

For in my calm, I find my grace,
I love this gentle, idle place.
Let the world run wild and crazy
I'll be here, proudly lazy.

They drone and nag in a single tone,
While I sit quiet, in peace, alone.
They frown at joy, at ease they scoff
Chasing storms, then running off.

Why the rush? What's all the fuss?
They've never just breathed like one of us.
No still mind, no inward sun...
They've never tried meditation, not once begun.

They said, "You're idle, your dream's asleep!"
But dreams like mine aren't sown that deep.
I smiled and answered, calm and clear,
"My dream is joy, and it's right here."

No need to chase, no frantic schemes
I'm living now within my dreams.
They call it lazy—let it be seen:
To rest in peace... is what I mean.

I sit, I stroll, I chill, I write,
In simple joys, I find my light.
They ask, "Why own not wealth or gold,
When you're so bright, so free, so bold?"

But I own peace, and that's my song,
I've known what's mine all along.
I'm lazy, yes it feels just right,
This life, this path, this gentle light.

They called me a couch potato, so bold,
But they never saw the peace I hold.
I wasn't lost I was gently seeking,
A soul like mine, calm and speaking.

Lazy me, lazy her our hearts align,
Together we found peace, so divine.
While they race and chase, their minds undone,
We're lazy, and in that, we've found our fun.

Paw-Paw

With four strong legs and a wagging tail,
They whisper stories, a timeless tale.
From pup to proud, they grow before your eyes,
Yet love you still, with no need for disguise.

Though words they lack, their love is clear,
With playful paws, they draw us near.
They nip, they chase, with boundless grace,
And greet us with a joyful face.

They sniff, they wag, with hearts so true,
No mask to wear, no lies to rue.
Their joy is pure, their spirits light,
Their eyes shine bright at every sight.

Wherever you lead, they gladly tread,
A loyal soul, by instinct led.
No voice they need, for love they show,
In every step, they let you know.

They came as strangers, quiet and shy,
Now stars that gleam in every eye.
More loyal than blood, truer at heart,
A bond so deep, no world could part.

They romp with heart by night and day,
They spring in laughter, free of fray.
Their innocence shines bright and keen,
No love purer than e'er we've seen.

They topple vases full of glee,
They shred our pants in playful spree.
They spring and bark with boundless sound,
Then sleep in peace when we're around.

Their adventures weave through every nook,
In every corner, their tales are hooked.
With muddy paws and fur that's matted,
The joy they've brought can never be fatted.

They race through fields, in sunlight's glow,
And dance in puddles, where wild winds blow.
Each wag, each bark, a memory made,
In every moment, their love won't fade.

Through storms they stay, with steadfast eyes,
A guardian spirit, where comfort lies.

With warmth they nestle, beside our side,
In their gentle presence, we take sweet pride.

Though seasons change and time may fleet,
Their heart remains a rhythmic beat.
With every glance, a promise shared,
In their loyal love, we are forever bared.

Unspoken Tongues

They spoke, yet I could not decode,
Their voices light, a fleeting road.
Let quiet moments softly bloom,
Where peace can chase away the gloom.
The world speaks in a thousand ways,
But soon I'll find the voice that stays.

They said that communication's the key,
Yet no door unlocked, no truth set free.
If it's merely a dialect we speak,
Why the struggle? Why the need to seek?

They spoke in tongues both sharp and strange,
Yet none in words the heart could range.
Each mind presumed the rest would know,
As if all truths in silence grow.

They thought their silence spoke to me,
A quiet truth I'd somehow see.
They hoped their hearts would be unmasked,

Yet never once was I truly asked.
I grasped the world's elusive thread,
But none heard what my insight said.

No voice spoke faith, no whisper hope,
No hand reached out with trust to cope.
No vow was made, no truth believed,
Just echoes shared, yet none received.
Still all aligned in silent rite,
Repeating tongues without the light.

In shadows cast, their faces fade,
As longing blooms in twilight's glade.
I wander through the unspoken fear,
Where dreams convene but never steer.

They spoke of bridges, yet built no ropes,
Just laughter tangled in fragile hopes.
Each gesture masked in riddles grand,
Yet understanding slipped through their hands.

The silence swells, a haunting swell,
A language woven, too deep to tell.
And as the night envelopes all,
I search for the echoes behind the wall.

What if a spark could light the dark?
Could hearts ignite from a single spark?
Still, I cling to the threads of fate,
In hopes of finding a voice to translate.

Dilema

They spoke, and I obeyed without a pause,
Their age, their wisdom was enough,
I thought their words were always true,
But truth was far, and doubt was due.

From lips to ears through time it spread,
A chain of thought the old ones fed,
Not wisdom's gift, but fear's disguise,
An embroidery of sacred lies.

They named it "culture," wrapped it tight,
A cloak that dimmed the clearest light.
Yet now I see through false traditions,
It's nothing more than superstitions.

"Don't go," they warned, "and don't you dare,
It's not the time, so don't go there."
The hours ruled by ancient rhyme,
Trapped within the myth of time.

I asked them "why?" with open eyes,
But silence came, no clear replies.
Just echoes wrapped in blind insistence,
A hollow voice of vague resistance.

I was young, yet they crowned me wise,
But chained my mind with old disguise.
Their morals tight, a heavy thread,
I questioned once, and stepped ahead.

I broke their rules, I spoke my flame,
To wake the ones who praised the same.
But wrath arose, a burning choir,
Their guilt was mine, their shame, my fire,

I tried so hard to make them see,
To lift them up, to set thought free.
I aimed for better, truth unsealed,
But they recoiled, their pride unrevealed.

"You know not," they said, with scornful air,
Yet once made me a wisdom heir.
If I know nothing then tell me when,
Why crown me once, then doubt me then?

One truth I learned, a quiet skill,
No need to lift the veil, nor fill
The gaps with tales they've yet to find
Let them seek, let them unwind.

No more to teach what we've been shown,
They'll learn the truths they've yet to own.

Sip Of Tea

Music played, the roads stretched wide,
She drove with me right by her side,
We journeyed on, the miles unspoken,
A sip of tea, our hearts unbroken.

Two young lovers in the twilight's glow,
Hand in hand, where time would flow,
We drove through hours, no end in sight,
A sip of tea, our hearts alight.

We spoke, we laughed, we argued too,
In every moment, we just knew,
No distance could ever tear us apart,
Yet a sip of tea, to soothe the heart.

Through highs and lows, with pockets light,
We spoke our truths, no need for flight,
She was herself, and I, just me,
Yet a sip of tea, we both did see.

The roads were rough, the bike was torn,
No other choice but to walk till dawn,
We geared up, we rose, and took the stride,
Without a sip of tea, none could guide.

A cloud so dark, they bade us wait,
But we were sparks, defying fate,
We kissed, we held, our hands entwined,
And whispered, "A sip of tea, then we'll return, aligned."

We talked, we dreamed, with plans in tow,
To fix the tire, still on the go,
He joked, she laughed — the stars would shine,
But we knew well: a sip of tea makes all things fine.

Same Clock, Same Chase

Woke to silence - my alarm had died,
Late again, no shock, no pride.
The streets yawn wide, a gray parade,
Each step rehearsed, each choice replayed.

Same old roads beneath my tread,
Same words, same desk, same overhead.
Nothing shifts, no winds arise,
Just ticking clocks and tired eyes.

A loop I trace from nine to five,
A fading echo, a worn-out line.
And yesterday still wears my name,
I'm just the same, the same, the same.

Another day slipped through my frame,
I stayed unchanged - just me to blame.
Each hour I gave to others' gain,
While dreams of mine slept still, in vain.

No spark for self, no climb, no claim,
I played it safe, I stayed the same.
A quiet fire I never named,
A life half-lived, a soul untamed.

I called it duty - they saw a chance,
To lead my steps, to make me dance.
My life, their game, their toy, their trick,
They knew just when to praise or kick.

Naive I was - the fault was mine,
Too blind to see the sly design.
I shone with fire, yet feared the flame,
Both cure and curse, they felt the same.

Nine to five - not just a role,
It swallowed years, it claimed my soul.
No dreams fulfilled, no mountains moved,
And sixty came - time never proved.

I gave no time for self or kin,
What's gained today can't heal where I've been.
A slave to life, to work, to strife,
No wealth or fame can fix my life.

Stop and pause - let go of gold,
If you can live with heart, not cold.

Your life, your choices, yours to take,
No blame, no claim, for your own sake.

Now I stand, the choice is mine,
To shape my fate, to cross the line.
No past to haunt, no chains to hold,
The future's mine, my story bold.

Worth Of She

She wore shorts, and eyes would stray,
She draped herself, yet eyes would play.
In doubt, she stood, unsure, unsure,
What to wear, what to endure.

The gaze, the judgment, heavy, cold,
Made her question what she'd been told.
What was her worth, when they just stared?
In their eyes, a truth laid bare.

She walked with pride, they called her vain,
She walked with doubt, they called her plain.
She learned and grew, a keeper's role,
Uneducated, still, they'd deem her soul.

She was but an object, held in men's eyes,
With many roles to play, yet still the same disguise.
Generations shifted, ideologies flew,
But she stayed the object, as if nothing new.

If she spoke with grace, they called her a game,
If she stayed silent, they questioned her name.
She walked with him - the whispers began,
She walked with her - still judged by man.

It wasn't her - the fault, not hers to bear,
But a world of judgments, harsh and unfair.
Not just by men, but by women grown old,
She was still the object, her story retold.

She showed them kindness, soft and true,
Yet the same old gaze still pierced right through.
No one stood guilty, none took the shame,
Except the one they made the name.

But she is not what the world defined,
Not just a body, nor weak of mind.
She rises now, with fire and grace,
No longer silent, she claims her space.

Their labels break on her iron will,
Their voices fade, yet she stands still.
She is the storm they tried to tame,
Not just a subject, she is the flame.

So let this echo, wide and far:
She is not less, she is the star.
No gaze, no name can cage her flight,
She owns her truth, She owns her light.

Beyond the day

A day arrived, a time to cheer,
But as the days slipped by, I lingered near.
Throughout the year, I stayed unseen,
A shadow in the crowd, lost in between.

"We're with you," they said, "we'll share your song,"
But as the moments passed, they proved me wrong.
In the end, when time had flown,
You turned away, and I stood alone.

Then came the parcels, dressed in hue,
I opened each but none rang true.
Polite words wrapped in ribboned guise,
I wondered, staring with weary eyes.

"If gifts must come, then why this day?
Why not a normal day?"
Where were they through all my days?
Why now this sudden, shallow praise?
I loved them true, if love was real,

Why wait for one set time to feel?

Love, a prisoner of a date,
Forced smiles cloaked a hollow fate.
Foolish heart, I played their game,
In the end, I bore the blame.

In love, she walked through all my dreams,
Each day we lived was lit with beams.
No need for dates to mark our way,
We found our joy in every day.

No clichés bound the love we knew,
No crafted lies, no staged ado.
Gifts came like whispers, soft and free,
Not chained to some set day's decree.

No story told for crowds to see,
Our love lived quiet, wild, and free.
No gifts to boast, no grand display,
Just whispered words along the way.

No need to shout, no need to prove,
A simple, soft "I love you" move.
A bond that bloomed without the guise,

Beneath the world's distracted eyes.

Silent witnesses of dying world

Once cradled by green, now towers rise tall,
Concrete jungles echo our own downfall.
We wrestle with troubles our hands have spun,
And curse the skies for what we've done.

The garden we knew lies barren and torn,
A wasteland where wild beauty was born.
Necessity's mask, this path we tread,
A world reshaped by hands we led.

We climb to the skies in towers of pride,
Seeking the green we've pushed aside.
Glass panes reveal not hills, but eyes!
A city of walls where freedom dies.

The breeze once danced through open land,
Now hums through vents at our command.
We speak of the children, the price they'll pay,
For choices we make today.

In comfort's name, we chased our thrill,
Now long for rains that once fell still.
We craft cool winds from iron and wire,
Yet stoke the flames of our own fire.

What once was mild, now scorches deep,
A restless heat we sowed in sleep.
Our thirst for ease, a bitter cost,
In seeking gain, so much was lost.

I once ran free on earthen land,
Now show my child a photo's stand.
The playground's gone, it sleeps below,
While kids in walls their childhood grow.

We feared the dirt, its stains, its grace
And lost the roots we can't replace.
In chasing clean, we left behind
The mess where joy and truth aligned.

Too late, perhaps, yet hope must stay,
Not words but acts must pave the way.
While nature gasps, we still debate
It's time to act before too late.

No more talks in quiet rooms,

But rise and move through gathering gloom.
Be not a speaker, but a spark
A voice that drives the needed mark.

As once said by a wise,
"I was cleaning the mirror for years, later came to know
that dirt was on my face"

Conversation with my younger self

My childhood ran with open arms,
A whisper soft, a soul unharmed.
Eyes wide with wonder, pure and free,
He said, "You once were wholly me."

No noise of doubt, no need to shout,
Just calm within and dreams throughout.
He asked of stars, of bugs, of sky,
And never once asked, "Who am I?"

He asked me, "Why did you outgrow?
Why cast me off, let silence grow?
Why press me down, why dim my light,
And hide me far from day and night?

Head bowed low, I wept in shame,
Embraced him close and took the blame.
"I dimmed your spark, I veiled your gleam,
I crushed your voice, I stole your dream."

I spoke, "No excuse, no defense to find,
The weight of my guilt pressed deep on my mind.
Chasing the dime, my own dream I'd trade,
Living for others, while my own life delayed."

He held my face within his hands,
Wiped my tears, and gave a smile that spans.
He said, "You worry too much, there's no need for fright,
Just live your truth, and everything will be right.

"Let's live as one, no wrong in sight,
Sometimes I'm you, and you're my light.
We'll chase today's dream, face tomorrow's fight,
With me in you, together we'll shine bright."

Now let us stand, both heart and soul,
To heal the wounds and make us whole.
We'll walk this path, both old and new,
The child in me will live in you.

So take my hand, let's journey far,
Chasing the moon, reaching for stars.
With every step, we'll find our way,
Together we'll rise, each night and day.

No longer lost, no longer torn,

The child's spirit forever reborn.
In each of us, the light will grow,
Together we're strong, together we glow

Echoes Of Quiet Journey

Amidst the rush, the long-awaited trip,
A chance to rest, to let our worries slip.
I packed too much, yet left some things behind,
And hand in hand, we journeyed, hearts aligned.

Tickets in hand, pockets light with glee,
We booked a car, to the airport, carefree.
With checks all done, we wandered around,
No treasures to buy, just passing the time 'til we're
bound.

We boarded the flight, she claimed the view,
I took her side, as the engines flew.
Attendants spoke, the journey took flight,
I felt the thrill, she gripped with slight fright.

All came to a halt as she gazed from the skies,
A sparkle lit up in her wide, wondering eyes.
Her jaw gently dropped, no words to convey,
Just pure, flowing joy that carried her away.

A stream down her cheek, like a soft summer rain,
In that fleeting moment, she was a child again.
The weight of the wait now made perfect sense,
A break long deserved, deep and immense.

As if the journey, not the end, was the key,
We drifted in awe, just her and me.
Our hearts ran wild, beyond our command,
No need for words, just a touch of her hand.

With stars in her eyes and a bright, bold grin,
She whispered, "Next time, we're doing this again."
We reached our stay, with hope held high,
A gentle pause beneath the sky.

We found our place and let time slow,
While golden light began to glow.
The window framed a dream so wide,
Where nature breathed in calm and pride.

So mild, so still it made us smile,
And hold that peace a little while.
We dashed outside, the door swung wide,
With laughs that echoed far and wide.

A snowy blanket kissed the ground,

While flakes like stars came drifting down.
The world aglow in silver light,
A glacier's fall within our sight.

So still, so pure, it caught our breath,
A quiet world where time knew death.
Our hands intertwined, away from the fray,
We left all behind, in this moment to stay.

Like children again, with snowman and fight,
Laughter and snowflakes, pure delight.
A break long awaited, a change so deep,
It brought us peace, a calm we'll keep.
In the quiet we found, with hearts full and free,
A tranquil new world where we could just be.